SPIRITUAL
NOURISHMENT

Thirty days of Bible verses
with words to nourish
and strengthen your faith

From the writings of Witness Lee & Watchman Nee

Living Stream Ministry
Anaheim, CA • www.lsm.org

Mass-distribution edition, August 2010.

ISBN 978-0-7363-4512-5

Free distribution by:
Bibles for America
P.O. Box 17537, Irvine, CA 92623 U.S.A.
www.bfa.org

See back page for distribution information.

Published by:
Living Stream Ministry
2431 W. La Palma Ave., Anaheim, CA 92801 U.S.A.
P.O. Box 2121, Anaheim, CA 92814 U.S.A.
www.lsm.org

Contents

Day	Topic
1	Man Having a Spirit to Contain God
2	The Woman and the Silver Coin
3	The Father and the Prodigal Son (1)
4	The Father and the Prodigal Son (2)
5	Where Does Faith Come From?
6	Obtaining Both Mercy and Grace
7	The Need for Confession
8	Standing on God's Side by Confessing Our Sins
9	Solving the Problem of Sin and Sins
10	Praising in the Midst of Any Situation
11	God Willingly Limiting Himself to Man's Free Will
12	Confessing Jesus Being to Call His Name
13	Grace Being with Our Spirit
14	Breathing by Calling
15	Loving God, the Indispensable Requirement
16	Peace Guarding Our Hearts
17	Christ as the Seed of Life Sown into the Believers
18	Mankind Being Created with a Spirit to Seek God
19	How Can Christ Be in Us?
20	Participating in the Lord's Riches
21	Receiving an Inheritance
22	Jesus Withstanding Temptations
23	Defeating the Devil as a Man
24	The Way to Defeat Satan (1)
25	The Way to Defeat Satan (2)
26	Touching the Untouchable
27	Our Need for the Divine Life
28	Faith, Love, and Peace (1)
29	Faith, Love, and Peace (2)
30	Faith, Love, and Peace (3)

Gen. 1:26 God said, Let Us make man in Our image, according to Our likeness...

Gen. 2:7, 9 Jehovah God formed man from the dust of the ground and breathed into his nostrils the breath of life, and man became a living soul...And out of the ground Jehovah God caused to grow every tree that is pleasant to the sight and good for food, as well as the tree of life in the middle of the garden...

1 Thes. 5:23 The God of peace Himself sanctify you wholly, and may your spirit and soul and body be preserved complete, without blame, at the coming of our Lord Jesus Christ.

WORDS OF MINISTRY: Genesis chapters 1 and 2 show us that when God created man, He made two preparations concerning man. The first preparation was that He created man in His image and according to His likeness. As man was created according to God, he resembles God in many aspects. The various aspects of man's expression, such as his pleasure, anger, sorrow, joy, preference, choice, etc.—whether it be his emotion, will, or disposition—express God to a certain degree and are miniatures of all that is in God.

Another preparation was that God created for man a spirit in the depths of his being. Of the countless varieties of living things in the universe, only man has a spirit. In the whole creation there is one kind of created being that is not spirit yet has a spirit, and that is man. Why did God create a spirit for man in the depths of his being? We all know that it was because God wants man to receive Him, who is Spirit. In the same way, He created a stomach for man because He wants man to take in food. Consider this: Suppose God did not create a stomach for man. How could we take in food? Because we have a stomach, we can receive food into us, enjoy it, digest it, and assimilate it into our being, making it our constituent. In the same manner, since we have a spirit within us, we can receive God into us and assimilate Him, making Him our very constituent.

In the first two chapters of Genesis, when God created man to be His vessel, He made these two steps of preparation: one step was to create man to be like Him, and the other was to put a spirit within man so that man might receive Him. After He had made these two preparations, He placed Himself before man in the form of the tree of life in order that man might receive Him and obtain Him as life. Brothers and sisters, it is in man's spirit that the contact between God and man is made. Once there is such a contact between God and man, God enters into man to be his content, and man becomes God's vessel to express Him outwardly. Thus God's eternal intention is fulfilled in man.

Witness Lee, *Lessons on Prayer*, pp. 14-15.
(Posted on www.emanna.com on 6/22/2002)

Luke 15:8-10 Or what woman having ten silver coins, if she loses one silver coin, does not light a lamp and sweep the house and seek carefully until she finds *it*? And when she finds *it*, she calls together her friends and neighbors, saying, Rejoice with me, for I have found the coin which I lost. In the same way, I tell you, there is joy in the presence of the angels of God over one sinner repenting.

WORDS OF MINISTRY: The lamp signifies the word of God (Psa. 119:105, 130) used by the Spirit to enlighten and expose the sinner's position and condition so that he may repent. As indicated by the parable of the seeking woman, the Spirit's work is to enlighten us inwardly. As this seeking woman, the Spirit enlightens our inner being little by little in a fine careful way. The Spirit enlightens our mind, then our emotion and will, and then our conscience and our entire heart. It is in this way that the Spirit "finds" us.

As the result of the Spirit's finding us through enlightening us, we wake up and come to ourselves and realize how foolish it is to stay where we are. We do not wake ourselves up; on the contrary, we are awakened by the enlightening of the seeking Spirit. This seeking, enlightening, and finding of the Spirit takes place neither in the wilderness nor on the cross; it happens in our heart. This results in repentance, which is a change in our mind that produces a change in the direction of our life.

The fact that the Spirit's finding us takes place within the "house" of our being reveals that we were lost in ourselves. We were lost in our mind, will, and emotion. We were not merely lost in the wilderness—we were lost in ourselves. Christ died on the cross to bring us back from the wilderness of the world, yet we remain lost in ourselves. Therefore, the Spirit finds us in ourselves. We can testify of this from our experience. When the Spirit enlightened our mind, emotion, will, conscience, and heart, then we began to repent.

This repentance resulting from the enlightening of the Spirit is altogether an inward matter. No human being and no angel is able to do such a subjective work in us. This can be done only by the penetrating Spirit, for the Spirit is able to penetrate the depths of our being to enlighten us and expose us. Then we realize how foolish we are, we repent, and we decide to come back to the Father.

Witness Lee, *Life-study of Luke,* pp. 292, 299.
(Posted on www.emanna.com on 2/8/2002)

Luke 15:11-20 He said, A certain man had two sons. And the younger of them said to the father, Father, give me the share of the estate that falls to *me*. And he distributed to them his living. And not many days after, the younger son, having gathered everything together, went abroad to a distant country and there squandered his estate by living dissolutely. And when he had spent all, a severe famine occurred throughout that country, and he began to be in want. And he went and joined himself to one of the citizens of that country; and he sent him into his fields to feed hogs. And he longed to be satisfied with the carob pods which the hogs were eating, and no one gave him *anything*. But when he came to himself, he said, How many of my father's hired servants abound in bread, but I am perishing here in famine! I will rise up and go to my father, and I will say to him, Father, I have sinned against heaven and before you. I am no longer worthy to be called your son; make me like one of your hired servants. And he rose up and came to his own father. But while he was still a long way off, his father saw him and was moved with compassion, and he ran and fell on his neck and kissed him affectionately.

WORDS OF MINISTRY: In verse 19 we see that the prodigal intended to say to his father, "I am no longer worthy to be called your son; make me like one of your hired servants." This indicates that the prodigal son did not know the father's love. A fallen sinner having once repented always thinks of working for God or serving God to obtain His favor, not knowing that this thought is against God's love and grace and is an insult to His heart and intent. The father's seeing the son did not happen by chance. Rather, the father went out of the home to look for his prodigal's return. When the father saw his son, he ran to him and fell on his neck and kissed him affectionately. This indicates that God the Father runs to receive a returning sinner. What eagerness this shows! The father's falling on his son's neck and kissing him affectionately shows a warm and loving reception.

If we read carefully the parable of the loving father, we shall see that while the prodigal son was still squandering the father's riches, the father was waiting for him to come back. When the son came to himself and decided to go to his father, he prepared what he would say to him: "Father, I have sinned against heaven and before you. I am no longer worthy to be called your son; make me like one of your hired servants" (vv. 18-19). What would you have said to the father if you had been the prodigal son in this parable? Perhaps you would have said to yourself, "I feel ashamed and foolish for squandering everything my father gave me. I cannot bear to recall the way I have been living. I know for sure that my father will not be outside waiting for me…"

To the prodigal son's great surprise, "while he was still a long way off, his father saw him and was moved with compassion, and he ran and fell on his neck and kissed him affectionately" (v. 20). Perhaps the prodigal said to himself, "This is like a dream! I didn't call out or knock on the door, but my father comes running to me. Now he is embracing me and kissing me!"

Witness Lee, *Life-study of Luke*, pp. 294, 300.
(Posted on www.emanna.com on 2/11/2002)

Luke 15:21-24 And the son said to him, Father, I have sinned against heaven and before you; I am no longer worthy to be called your son. But the father said to his slaves, Bring out quickly the best robe and put *it* on him, and put a ring on his hand and sandals on his feet. And bring the fattened calf; slaughter *it*, and let us eat and be merry, because this son of mine was dead and lives again; he was lost and has been found. And they began to be merry.

WORDS OF MINISTRY: When the son returned home, he was a poor beggar dressed in rags. But after the best robe was put on him, he was covered with a splendid garment prepared especially for him. With this robe on, he was qualified to match his father. The best robe put on the son is a full type of Christ as our righteousness in whom we are justified before God. Hence, putting the best robe on the returned prodigal signifies justification in Christ. As those who have Christ as the best robe, we are justified by God.

The father also told the slaves to put a ring on his son's hand. I believe this was a gold ring. This ring signifies the sealing Spirit given to a returned sinner (Eph. 1:13). This ring is a sign that a repentant sinner receives something divine, the very Spirit of God Himself. The ring signifying the sealing Spirit indicates that the returned prodigal belongs to the Father. It also indicates that whatever the Father has as an inheritance belongs to the returned son.

In 15:22 we see that sandals were also put on the feet of the returned son. Sandals separate one's feet from the dirt of the earth and strengthen him for walking. The sandals put on the son's feet signify that God's salvation separates us from the world and unto Him so that we may then take His way.

With the robe, the ring, and the sandals the returned one was fully clothed and adorned. This means that he was fully justified and qualified and could be accepted into the father's house. Then the father told the slaves to bring the fattened calf and slaughter it for their enjoyment. Thus far, we see Christ as righteousness to justify a repentant sinner outwardly, the Spirit as the seal, and the power of God's salvation separating a repentant sinner from the world. Now we see that Christ is also the fattened calf to fill us with the divine life for our enjoyment. The father, the returned son, and all the others could enjoy feasting on this fattened calf. So "they began to be merry."

Witness Lee, *Life-study of Luke*, pp. 301-302.
(Posted on www.emanna.com on 2/12/2002)

Rom. 3:22 Even the righteousness of God through the faith of Jesus Christ to all those who believe...

Heb. 12:2 Looking away unto Jesus, the Author and Perfecter of our faith...

WORDS OF MINISTRY: We believe in Jesus Christ by His faith, for we have no faith of our own. Jesus is the Author and Perfecter of our faith. The more we look at ourselves and examine ourselves, the faster our faith disappears. Faith is not our invention; it can never be initiated by us. It is impossible for us to generate faith. If you look at yourself, you will never find faith, but if you forget about yourself and say, "O Lord Jesus, I love You," faith will immediately rise up within you. This faith is the faith of Jesus, or we may say that it is Jesus believing within us. Thus, the phrase *through the faith of Jesus Christ* means believing in Jesus Christ by His faith.

The righteousness of God has been manifested apart from the law by our believing in Jesus Christ by His faith. We believe in Christ by His faith, not by our own faith. Christ is our faith. Never say that you cannot believe, for you can believe if you want to. Do not try to believe by yourself, because the more you try, the less faith you have. Simply say, "O Lord Jesus, I love You. Lord Jesus, You are so good." If you do this, you will have faith immediately. We believe in Jesus Christ by His faith, and out of this faith and to this faith the righteousness of God is revealed to all who believe.

Witness Lee, *Life-study of Romans*, p. 58.
(Posted on www.emanna.com on 8/4/2004)

Rom. 9:15 ..."I will have mercy on whomever I will have mercy, and I will have compassion on whomever I will have compassion."

Rom. 11:5 In the same way then at the present time also there has come into being a remnant according to the selection of grace.

WORDS OF MINISTRY: It is somewhat difficult to understand mercy and grace as they are related to God's selection. Although we were selected and foreknown by God in eternity past, when God came to call us, we were in a pitiful situation, a situation that required God's mercy. The enemy, the devil, might have said to God, "Look at this one who is Your selection. How pitiful he is!" Then God might have said to Satan, "Satan, don't you realize that this is a very good opportunity for Me to show My mercy? Without such a pitiful person, how could I show My mercy? If everyone were perfect and up to your standard, I would have no one on whom to show mercy. Satan, this chosen one is the right one to be the object of My mercy."

What about grace? As we have seen, grace is something of God wrought into our being. We are not only the objects of God's mercy; we are also the objects of His grace. We are under God's mercy, and His grace is within us. We all can testify that though we were most pitiful and miserable, God came in and granted us His mercy, and we repented. At that very time, something divine—God's grace—was wrought into us. Now we are not only under God's mercy; we also have His grace, the living person of Christ as the Spirit, within us. This is God's selection.

Witness Lee, *Life-study of Genesis,* p. 865.
(Posted on www.emanna.com on 3/10/2007)

1 John 1:7, 9 If we walk in the light as He is in the light, we have fellowship with one another, and the blood of Jesus His Son cleanses us from every sin...If we confess our sins, He is faithful and righteous to forgive us our sins and cleanse us from all unrighteousness.

WORDS OF MINISTRY: Believers are the children of light and the children of God (1 John 3:1). You are a child of God, and you should know sin. You should have the same attitude toward sin as your Father. Confession in God's house comes when His children take the same attitude as their Father toward sin. They condemn sin in the same way that their Father condemns sin.

If we confess our sins this way, God "is faithful and righteous to forgive us our sins and cleanse us from all unrighteousness." When we sin and when we know our sin and acknowledge it as sin, God will forgive us our sin and cleanse us from all unrighteousness. God is "faithful," which means that He must honor and fulfill His own words and promises. He is also "righteous," which means that He must be satisfied with His Son's redemptive work on the cross and must recognize it. Based on His promise and based on His redemption, He has to forgive us. He is faithful, and He is righteous. He must forgive us our sins and cleanse us from all unrighteousness.

We have to pay attention to the words *every* and *all* in 1 John 1:7 and 9. "Every sin" and "all unrighteousness" are fully forgiven and cleansed. The Lord has done this. When the Lord says all, He means all. We should never change it to something else. When He says every sin, He means every sin, not just every sin committed before we believed or every sin committed in the past. He has forgiven us of all sins.

Watchman Nee, *The Collected Works of Watchman Nee*, vol. 49, *Messages for Building Up New Believers (2)*, pp. 329-330.
(Posted on www.emanna.com on 4/28/2001)

Standing on God's Side
by Confessing Our Sins

1 John 1:9 If we confess our sins, He is faithful and righteous to forgive us our sins and cleanse us from all unrighteousness.

WORDS OF MINISTRY: In this verse the word *we* refers to believers, not to sinners. When a believer sins, he must confess his sins. Only after he has confessed his sins will he be forgiven. When a believer sins, he should not ignore it or cover it up. Proverbs 28:13 says, "He who covers his transgressions will not prosper / But whoever confesses and forsakes them will obtain mercy." Do not give sin a nice name. Do not excuse yourself. Lying is a sin. When you lie, you should confess that you have sinned. You should not say, "I have said a little more (or less) than I should have." You should say, "I have sinned." You should not explain it away or cover it up. You should confess that you have committed the sin of lying. You must condemn lying as sin.

Once we sin, we are away from God. Once we join ourselves to sins, we cannot be together with God. As soon as Adam sinned, he hid from God and dared not meet Him (Gen. 3:8). Colossians 1:21 says, "You, though once alienated and enemies in your mind because of your evil works." Sin alienates us from God. What does it mean to confess our sins? It means to come back to God's side and to acknowledge that what we have done is sin. We have come back to God. We are no longer with sin. We are standing opposite of sin and calling sin a sin. This is confession. Only those who walk in the light and who have deep feelings and a repulsion for sin can have genuine confession. Those who are callous to sin, who consider it natural to sin, are not making any confession when they merely acknowledge something with their lips in a heartless way.

Watchman Nee, *The Collected Works of Watchman Nee*, vol. 49, *Messages for Building Up New Believers (2)*, pp. 328-329.
(Posted on www.emanna.com on 4/27/2001)

Rom. 5:18–19 So then as it *was* through one offense unto condemnation to all men, so also *it was* through one righteous act unto justification of life to all men. For just as through the disobedience of one man [Adam] the many were constituted sinners, so also through the obedience of the One [Jesus Christ] the many will be constituted righteous.

WORDS OF MINISTRY: All our sins were put on the Man-Savior. The root of our sins is the sin that came into mankind from Satan. This sin indwells us. When our sins were put on the Lord Jesus, He was made the very sin that indwells us. Therefore, both the root—indwelling sin—and the fruit—our sins—were put upon Him. As such a One, He was judged by God according to His righteousness.

First Corinthians 15:3 says, "Christ died for our sins." First Peter 2:24 tells us that He Himself "bore up our sins in His body on the tree." These verses indicate that Christ bore our sins and died for them. Hebrews 9:28 says that Christ was "offered once to bear the sins of many," and verse 26 in the same chapter says, "He has been manifested for the putting away of sin through the sacrifice of Himself." Both sin and sins were dealt with by His death once for all. Therefore, we may call His death an eternal death, a once-for-all death.

When the Lord Jesus was bearing our sins and was made sin on the cross, He was considered by God to be the Lamb of God. "Behold, the Lamb of God, who takes away the sin of the world!" (John 1:29). In this verse the *world* refers to mankind, to the human race. The Lamb of God took away the sin of mankind. The problem of sin has been solved by His vicarious death for us.

Witness Lee, *Life-study of Luke*, pp. 454-455.
(Posted on www.emanna.com on 5/10/2002)

Praising in the Midst of Any Situation

Psa. 9:1–2 I will give thanks to You, O Jehovah, with all my heart; / I will tell out all Your wonders. / I will rejoice and exult in You; / I will sing psalms to Your name, O Most High.

Psa. 119:164 Seven times a day I praise You / For Your righteous ordinances.

WORDS OF MINISTRY: David said in a psalm that he prayed to God three times a day. Yet in another psalm, he said that he praised God seven times a day. David was inspired by the Holy Spirit when he acknowledged the importance of praising. He prayed only three times a day, but he praised seven times a day.

The book of Psalms is full of praises. The book of Psalms is in fact a book of praise in the Old Testament. Many praises are quoted from Psalms. However, the Psalms contain chapters not only of praises but also of suffering. God wants His people to know that the praising ones are the very ones who have been led through trying situations and whose feelings have been wounded. These psalms show us men led by God through shadows of darkness. They were rejected, slandered, and persecuted. Words of praise do not always come from the mouths of the smooth-sailing ones. They come much more from those who are under discipline and trial. In the Psalms we can touch the most wounded feelings, and in the Psalms we also can find the greatest and highest praises. God uses many hardships, difficulties, and slanders to create praises in His people. He causes them to learn through difficult circumstances to become praising persons before the Lord.

Watchman Nee, *The Collected Works of Watchman Nee*, vol. 48, *Messages for Building Up New Believers (1)*, pp. 247-248.
(Posted on www.emanna.com on 10/5/2001)

Gen. 2:8-9 Jehovah God planted a garden in Eden, in the east; and there He put the man whom He had formed. And out of the ground Jehovah God caused to grow every tree that is pleasant to the sight and good for food, as well as the tree of life in the middle of the garden and the tree of the knowledge of good and evil.

Deut. 30:19 I call heaven and earth to witness against you today: I have set before you life and death, blessing and curse; therefore choose life that you and your seed may live.

WORDS OF MINISTRY: Some may ask why God would want the earth to control heaven. There is an eternity past and an eternity future. Between these two eternities, there is time. Within this section called time, God is limited. He cannot work as freely as He wants to. This is a limitation that God encountered in the creation of man. According to Genesis 2, God gave man a free will when He created him. God has a will, and man has a will. Whenever man's will is not one with God's will, God is limited.

If the earth was filled with spiritless material, God would be without restriction. But one day God created man. The man He created was not like a piece of stone or wood; he was not a table or a chair that could be placed here or there by God at will. The man that God created had a free will. Man could choose to obey God's word, and he also could choose to disobey His word. God did not create a man who was obligated to obey Him. He created a man with a free will, one who could obey or disobey His word. After God created man with a free will, His power was limited by this man. He could no longer act according to what He wanted. He had to ask whether man wanted the same thing and whether he was willing to do the same thing. God cannot treat man like a stone, a piece of wood, a table, or a chair, because man has a free will. Since the day God created man,

man could choose to allow God's authority to be carried out or to be blocked. This is why we say that within time, the period between the two eternities, God's authority is limited by man.

God is willing to be limited in time because He wants to gain a harmonious will in the second eternity. He wants man's free will to be harmonious with His will. This is a glory to God. God does not want the man He created to be like a book that can be shuffled around at will. Even though God wants man to be fully submissive to Him, He also gave man a free will. God's intention is that man's free will would choose to obey Him. This is a glory to God! In eternity future the free will of man will be joined to God's eternal will. That will be the time for God's eternal will to be fulfilled and for man's free will to become harmonious with God's eternal will.

Watchman Nee, *The Collected Works of Watchman Nee*, vol. 22, *The Assembly Life & The Prayer Ministry of the Church*, pp. 140-141.
(Posted on www.emanna.com on 6/27/2002)

Phil. 2:10–11 That in the name of Jesus every knee should bow, of those who are in heaven and on earth and under the earth, and every tongue should openly confess that Jesus Christ is Lord to the glory of God the Father.

Rom. 10:12 For there is no distinction between Jew and Greek, for the same Lord *is Lord* of all *and* rich to all who call upon Him.

WORDS OF MINISTRY: In the name of Jesus every knee will bow, and every tongue will openly confess that Jesus Christ is Lord. This implies calling on the name of the Lord. When we call on the Lord's name, we have the reality of bowing our knees to Him. Paul's word about bowing our knees in verse 10 and confessing in verse 11 implies that as we bow our knees to the Lord, we call on His name. We confess the Lord's name openly by calling on Him.

We have pointed out again and again that Philippians is a book on the experience of Christ. Calling on the name of the Lord Jesus is a way to experience Him and enjoy Him. Many of us can testify that before we began to call on the Lord's name, we did not have much experience of Him or enjoyment of Him. But when we call on the Lord, we spontaneously exercise our spirit and thereby touch the Lord who dwells in our spirit. As the life-giving Spirit in our spirit, the Lord is the fresh spiritual air for our enjoyment and experience. Many of us can testify how much we enjoy Him by calling on His name. Just as it is very helpful to breathe deeply of fresh air for the cleansing of our system, so we need to breathe deeply of the spiritual air by calling on the name of the Lord. By calling on the name of the Lord Jesus, we are stirred in spirit and even set on fire. Let us all learn to call, "O Lord Jesus," from the depths of our being. In this way we shall worship the Lord and openly confess Him.

Witness Lee, *Life-study of Philippians*, pp. 99-100.
(Posted on www.emanna.com on 10/23/2002)

Phil. 4:23 The grace of the Lord Jesus Christ be with your spirit.

2 Tim. 4:22 The Lord be with your spirit. Grace be with you.

John 3:6 That which is born of the flesh is flesh, and that which is born of the Spirit is spirit.

WORDS OF MINISTRY: When Paul says, "The grace of the Lord Jesus Christ be with your spirit," he means that the supply and enjoyment of the Triune God by and through the bountiful supply of the Spirit of Jesus Christ should be with us. When we have such a supply, we enjoy and experience the Triune God all day long. The spirit here is our regenerated spirit indwelt by the Spirit of Christ. It is in this spirit of ours that we enjoy Christ and experience Him as Paul did. Many Christians today have missed the mark of the regenerated spirit. They speak much about the Holy Spirit, but not of the human spirit. Because of this neglect of the regenerated human spirit, there is very little experience of Christ or enjoyment of the all-inclusive grace.

If we would enjoy the grace which is with our spirit, we need to exercise our spirit. The way to exercise the spirit is to pray, pray-read the Word, and call on the name of the Lord Jesus. Whenever we call on the Lord Jesus or pray to God the Father, we automatically exercise our spirit…When we call on the Lord, pray in a proper way, and pray-read the Word, we truly exercise our spirit. Exercising our spirit in this way is the secret to enjoying the grace which is with our spirit. Oh, we all need more exercise of the spirit to enjoy the Lord!

We know that man has three parts: the spirit, the soul, and the body. Bodily exercise is necessary and profitable. When I exercise physically, I sleep better at night. It is hardly necessary to speak of the exercise of the soul, especially of the mind, since this is emphasized so much in the schools. But there is a great need to emphasize the need to exercise the spirit. The more we exercise the spirit, the more we shall be healthy and strong in our entire being. Our physical body will be healthy, our mind will be sober and keen, and our spirit will be energized. Again I say, the exercise of the spirit is the secret, the unique way, to participate in the very grace which is the Triune God as the all-inclusive Spirit. As we enjoy Him, we become healthy and strong in our spirit and in our whole being.

Witness Lee, *Life-study of Philippians*, pp. 270-272.
(Posted on www.emanna.com on 2/19/2003)

1 Thes. 5:17-19 Unceasingly pray, in everything give thanks; for this is the will of God in Christ Jesus for you. Do not quench the Spirit.

WORDS OF MINISTRY: In 1 Thessalonians 5:17 Paul charges us to pray without ceasing. What does it mean to pray unceasingly? Although we may eat several meals a day and although we may drink many times during the day, no one can eat and drink without ceasing. But we certainly breathe unceasingly. Paul's command to pray without ceasing implies that unceasing prayer is like breathing. But how can our prayer become our spiritual breathing? How can we turn prayer into breathing? The way to do this is to call on the name of the Lord. We need to call on the Lord Jesus continually. This is the way to breathe, to pray without ceasing. Because we are not accustomed to this, we need to practice calling on the Lord's name all the time. To live is to breathe. Spiritually speaking, to breathe is to call on the Lord's name and to pray. By calling on the name of the Lord Jesus, we breathe the Spirit.

After Paul charges us to pray without ceasing and to give thanks in everything, he tells us not to quench the Spirit (v. 19). This indicates that if we do not pray and give thanks, we quench the Spirit. To stop praying is to stop breathing. Thus, to quench the Spirit is to cease from breathing.

All day long, no matter where we are or what we are doing, we need to call on the Lord. Whatever we are doing, we should call on the Lord Jesus. Call on the Lord's name in every situation, even when you are about to lose your temper. By calling on the Lord, you will live Christ. However, if you make up your mind not to lose your temper, you will be defeated. Your temper will be worse. Instead of trying to control your temper, turn to the Lord and call on Him. Say, "Lord Jesus, I love You. Lord, I am going to lose my temper. Be one with me in this." If you do this, you will be saved from your temper, and you will live Christ.

Witness Lee, *Life-study of Philippians*, pp. 298-299.
(Posted on www.emanna.com on 2/25/2003)

Rom. 8:28 We know that all things work together for good to those who love God...

1 Cor. 2:9 As it is written, "Things which eye has not seen and ear has not heard and *which* have not come up in man's heart; things which God has prepared for those who love Him."

WORDS OF MINISTRY: God does not alter things; He changes your heart. If you love God, then all things, though unaltered, will work for your good. Sometimes you complain about everything that comes your way. You complain concerning this and concerning that. Yet if love is there, all these will mean nothing to you. Loving God will make an unsatisfactory environment a profitable one.

To realize and participate in the deep and hidden things God has ordained and prepared for us requires us not only to believe in Him but also to love Him. To fear God, to worship God, and to believe in God (that is, to receive God) are all inadequate; to love Him is the indispensable requirement. To love God means to set our entire being—spirit, soul, and body, with the heart, soul, mind, and strength (Mark 12:30)—absolutely on Him, that is, to let our entire being be occupied by Him and lost in Him, so that He becomes everything to us and we are one with Him practically in our daily life. In this way we have the closest and most intimate fellowship with God, and we are able to enter into His heart and apprehend all its secrets. Thus, we not only realize but also experience, enjoy, and fully participate in these deep and hidden things of God.

Watchman Nee, *The Collected Works of Watchman Nee*, vol. 18, *Notes on Scriptural Messages (2)*, pp. 359-360; and Witness Lee, footnote 3 of 1 Corinthians 2:9 in the Recovery Version of the Bible.
(Posted on www.emanna.com on 5/3/2003)

Phil. 4:6-7 In everything, by prayer and petition with thanksgiving, let your requests be made known to God; and the peace of God, which surpasses every *man's* understanding, will guard your hearts and your thoughts in Christ Jesus.

WORDS OF MINISTRY: What will be the result if we let our requests be made known to God in everything by prayer and petition with thanksgiving? There will be the best result. The word *guard* in the original language is a special military term. We can translate it as "garrison" or "patrol." God's peace is patrolling our heart like the soldiers garrisoning the city, and His peace is keeping our heart in peace. No anxiety can break through this line and come into our heart. How amazing this is!

According to our concept, as soon as man sinned, God should have sent forth the Savior. But God was not anxious. When the fullness of the time came, God sent forth His Son. He waited several thousand years; He was not in a hurry. Even if men attack Him, oppose Him, and deny Him, He does not send thunder and lightning to kill them. He is at peace. Although He encounters many adversities, He is still very much at peace.

God has commanded that we should let our requests be made known to Him in everything through prayer and petition with thanksgiving. He has promised that He will send us His own peace like soldiers guarding our hearts, keeping out all worries, sufferings, and discomforts. If we commit everything to Him, we will have the peace which is beyond human understanding and which man cannot otherwise possess. This peace will guard our hearts and thoughts and enable us to safely pass through every storm in the worldly sea. You will be surprised, and others will marvel at your peace.

Watchman Nee, *The Collected Works of Watchman Nee*, vol. 18, *Notes on Scriptural Messages (2)*, pp. 262-264.
(Posted on www.emanna.com on 8/17/2004)

Christ as the Seed of Life Sown into the Believers

Acts 14:22 Establishing the souls of the disciples, exhorting *them* to continue in the faith and *saying* that through many tribulations we must enter into the kingdom of God.

1 Pet. 1:23 Having been regenerated not of corruptible seed but of incorruptible, through *the* living and abiding word of God.

WORDS OF MINISTRY: The kingdom of God was a main subject of the apostles' preaching in Acts. It is not a material kingdom visible to human sight, but a kingdom of the divine life. It is the spreading of Christ as life to His believers to form a realm in which God rules in His life. According to the New Testament, the kingdom of God is not a visible, material realm. Actually, the kingdom of God is a person, the Lord Jesus Christ Himself. When He was questioned by the Pharisees about the kingdom, "He answered them and said, The kingdom of God does not come with observation; nor will they say, Behold, here it is! or, There! For behold, the kingdom of God is in the midst of you" (Luke 17:20-21). As the context proves, the kingdom of God is the Savior Himself, who was among the Pharisees. Wherever the Savior is, there is the kingdom of God. This was the reason He could say that the kingdom was in the midst of the Pharisees. As the Lord's word indicates, this kingdom does not come with observation; that is, it is spiritual, not material and visible. In the four Gospels the Lord Jesus sowed Himself as the seed of the kingdom into His disciples. The development of this kingdom seed begins in Acts and continues in all the Epistles. This development reaches its consummation—the harvest—in the book of Revelation. The kingdom is Christ as the seed sown into the hearts of His chosen people. Our hearts are the soil into which the kingdom seed is sown and in which this seed develops. This is the proper definition of the kingdom of God.

Witness Lee, *Life-study of Acts,* pp. 342-343.
(Posted on www.emanna.com on 3/30/2007)

Mankind Being Created
with a Spirit to Seek God

Acts 17:16, 27 While Paul was waiting for them in Athens, his spirit was provoked within him as he beheld that the city was full of idols…That they might seek God, if perhaps they might grope for Him and find *Him*, even though He is not far from each one of us.

WORDS OF MINISTRY: Acts 17:16 says, "While Paul was waiting for them in Athens, his spirit was provoked within him as he beheld that the city was full of idols." The *spirit* here was Paul's human spirit (Job 32:8; Prov. 20:27), regenerated by the Spirit of God (John 3:6), indwelt by the Lord the Spirit (2 Tim. 4:22; Rom. 8:10-11), and acting with the Spirit (Rom. 8:16), in which Spirit he worshipped and served God (John 4:24; Rom. 1:9). Such a spirit was provoked by the many idols in Athens. Even the highest culture did not prevent the people in Athens from worshipping idols, because within them, as within all mankind, was a God-worshipping spirit created by God for man to seek and worship Him. However, due to their blindness and ignorance, they took the wrong objects for their worship (Acts 17:23). Now the true God, who created the universe and them, sent His apostle to announce the true object whom they should worship. Why was idol worship prevailing in Athens, the most cultured city? The reason is that in every human being there is a God-seeking and God-worshipping spirit. Of course, many do not seek the true God or worship the true God. Instead, they have the wrong object of worship. Nevertheless, the fact that people worship something or are seeking something to worship is a strong proof that man needs God. There is a need in man, especially in man's spirit, for God as the true object of worship.

Witness Lee, *Life-study of Acts*, pp. 398-399.
(Posted on www.emanna.com on 4/9/2007)

John 14:16-18, 20 I will ask the Father, and He will give you another Comforter...*even* the Spirit of reality...I will not leave you *as* orphans; I am coming to you...In that day you will know that I am in My Father, and you in Me, and I in you.

WORDS OF MINISTRY: How can Christ be in us? Christ is in us because of resurrection. Because the Lord Jesus has resurrected and because He is now in the Holy Spirit, He can be in us...If the Lord Jesus were not a resurrected Lord, if He were only a Lord who once lived on the earth, He could only be Himself forever, while I could only be myself forever. There would be no way for us to receive Him. It would not matter how holy and lovely Jesus of Nazareth was; there would be no way for us to receive Him, because He would only be a man. But thank the Lord that He is not only a man today; He has died and resurrected. In the Holy Spirit, He has become the Lord whom we can receive.

The Holy Spirit is the Lord's coming in another form. Another name for the Holy Spirit is "the Spirit of Jesus." He is also called "the Spirit of Christ." When the Lord put on the Holy Spirit, He became a "receivable" Lord. If He had not become such a Lord, we would not be able to enjoy Him. Christ has resurrected and put on the Holy Spirit. When we receive the Holy Spirit, we receive Christ; in the same way, when we receive the Son, we receive the Father. The Lord Jesus has resurrected, and He is in the Holy Spirit. Therefore, we can receive Him into us to be our life.

Watchman Nee, *The Collected Works of Watchman Nee,* vol. 36, *Central Messages,* pp. 170-171.
(Posted on www.emanna.com on 11/30/2000)

Rom. 10:8, 12-13 But what does it say? "The word is near you, in your mouth and in your heart," that is, the word of the faith which we proclaim...For there is no distinction between Jew and Greek, for the same Lord *is Lord* of all *and* rich to all who call upon Him; for "whoever calls upon the name of the Lord shall be saved."

WORDS OF MINISTRY: I had been told that whoever calls on the name of the Lord will be saved, but I had never heard that the Lord is rich to all who call on His name. He is rich not only in initial salvation—He is rich in all divine and spiritual things. If we would participate in the Lord's riches, we need to call on Him. Day and night, we should call on the name of the Lord. Although we may call quietly so as not to disturb others, we can still softly call, "O Lord Jesus." How do we know that the Lord is near us? We know this by calling on the Lord. You cannot convince someone that the Lord is near him by arguing or debating with him. The more we argue, the farther away the Lord may seem to be. But if instead of arguing we call on His name a few times, we shall sense that He is near. If we continue calling on Him, we shall realize that He is not only near but even within us. The more we call on the Lord, the more He becomes our enjoyment. Through calling on Him He also becomes our peace, rest, comfort, and solution in all kinds of situations. This is not a mere doctrine or superficial teaching; this is a truth for our experience.

Witness Lee, *Life-study of Acts,* pp. 537-538.
(Posted on www.emanna.com on 5/9/2007)

Acts 26:18 To open their eyes, to turn *them* from darkness to light and *from* the authority of Satan to God, that they may receive forgiveness of sins and an inheritance among those who have been sanctified by faith in Me.

Col. 1:12 Giving thanks to the Father, who has qualified you for a share of the allotted portion of the saints in the light.

WORDS OF MINISTRY: As the result of having our eyes opened and of being transferred from the authority of Satan to God, we not only have the forgiveness of sins on the negative side, but also we receive an inheritance on the positive side. This divine inheritance is the Triune God Himself with all that He has, all that He has done, and all that He will do for His redeemed people. This Triune God is embodied in the all-inclusive Christ (Col. 2:9), who is the portion allotted to the saints as their inheritance (1:12). The Holy Spirit, who has been given to the saints, is the foretaste, the seal, the pledge, and the guarantee of this divine inheritance (Eph. 1:13-14), which we are sharing and enjoying today in God's New Testament jubilee as a foretaste and will share and enjoy in full in the coming age and for eternity (1 Pet. 1:4). In the type of the jubilee in Leviticus 25:8-13, the main blessings were the liberty proclaimed and the returning of every man unto his own inheritance. In the fulfillment of the jubilee here, liberation from the authority of darkness and receiving the divine inheritance are also the primary blessings. In the Old Testament the twelve tribes of Israel each received an allotment, a portion, of the good land for an inheritance. The good land is a type of the all-inclusive Christ given to us as our inheritance. Therefore, Christ, the embodiment of the processed Triune God, is our inheritance.

Witness Lee, *Life-study of Acts,* pp. 602-603.
(Posted on www.emanna.com on 5/17/2007)

Luke 4:1 Jesus, full of the Holy Spirit, returned from the Jordan and was led by the Spirit in the wilderness, while being tempted for forty days by the devil.

Matt. 4:1 Then Jesus was led up into the wilderness by the Spirit to be tempted by the devil.

WORDS OF MINISTRY: After being baptized in water and anointed with the Spirit of God, Jesus as a man moved according to the leading of the Spirit. First of all, the Spirit led the anointed Man-Savior to be tempted by the devil. This temptation was a test to prove that He was qualified to be the Man-Savior. In Matthew 6:13 the Lord Jesus taught the disciples to pray, "Do not bring us into temptation." The Lord, however, was led by the Holy Spirit into the wilderness in order that He might be tempted by the devil. The Lord Jesus was strong, and He could withstand temptation. We, on the contrary, are not able to withstand temptation at all. The Lord Jesus is the only One who can stand the temptation of God's enemy. When He was on earth, He was perfect and strong. Therefore, the Holy Spirit, who is God reaching man, led this perfect man into temptation in order to defeat God's enemy…We are not able to withstand the temptation of the evil one. Therefore we need to pray, "O Father, do not lead me into temptation." No matter how strong we may feel, we actually are weak and cannot withstand Satan's temptation. The only One in this universe with the humanity that can withstand the temptation of God's enemy is the Lord Jesus, our Man-Savior.

Witness Lee, *Life-study of Luke*, pp. 76-77.
(Posted on www.emanna.com on 6/28/2007)

Luke 4:2-4 He did not eat anything in those days, and when they were concluded, He became hungry. And the devil said to Him, If You are the Son of God, speak to this stone that it become bread. And Jesus answered him, It is written, "Man shall not live on bread alone."

WORDS OF MINISTRY: For the Lord Jesus to accomplish His ministry, He had to defeat God's enemy, the devil, Satan. This He had to do as a man. Hence, He stood as a man to confront the enemy of God. The devil, knowing this, tempted Him to leave the standing of man and assume His position as the Son of God. Forty days before, God the Father declared from the heavens that Jesus was the beloved Son of the Father. The subtle tempter took that declaration as the ground to tempt the Lord Jesus. If the Lord assumed His position as the Son of God before the enemy, He would have lost the standing to defeat him. To cause a stone to become bread would certainly have been a miracle. That was proposed by the devil as a temptation. Many times the thought of having a miracle performed in certain situations is a temptation from the devil. The devil tempted the Man-Savior to take His position as the Son of God. But the Lord Jesus answered by saying, "Man shall not live on bread alone." This indicates that He stood in the position of man to deal with the enemy. The demons addressed Jesus as the Son of God (Matt. 8:29), but the evil spirits do not confess that Jesus Christ has come in the flesh (1 John 4:3), because in confessing Jesus as a man they admit that they are defeated. Although the demons confess Jesus as the Son of God, the devil does not want people to believe that He is the Son of God, because in so believing they will be saved (John 20:31).

Witness Lee, *Life-study of Luke*, pp. 77-78.
(Posted on www.emanna.com on 6/29/2007)

The Way to Defeat Satan (1)

Gen. 1:26 God said, Let Us make man in Our image, according to Our likeness...

Gen. 2:9 Out of the ground Jehovah God caused to grow every tree that is pleasant to the sight and good for food, as well as the tree of life in the middle of the garden...

Gen. 3:1 Now the serpent was more crafty than any *other* animal of the field...And he said to the woman...

WORDS OF MINISTRY: In Genesis 1 we have the man created by God in His image. For man to be created in God's image means that man is created according to God's attributes. God is love and light, and He is also holy and righteous. Love, light, holiness, and righteousness are God's attributes, and God created man according to these attributes. However, the man created by God in Genesis 1 merely bore God's image. He did not have God within him. Hence, he was merely a God-created man; he was not yet a God-man. Because God wanted the man created by Him to become a God-man, after creating man God placed him in front of the tree of life. The tree of life denotes God. God's intention was that the man created by Him would receive Him, as signified by the tree of life, and thereby become a God-man. However, the created man failed in that he did not receive the tree of life. Because man did not partake of the tree of life, he remained simply a God-created man. In Genesis 3 the enemy, the tempter, came in to tempt the man God had created. Because man had not become a God-man, because he did not actually have God within him, he was not able to withstand the enemy's temptation. The reason Adam could not withstand the temptation was that he was merely a God-created man, not a God-man. It is very important for us to see this.

Witness Lee, *Life-study of Luke*, p. 84.
(Posted on www.emanna.com on 6/30/2007)

Matt. 1:20 Do not be afraid to take Mary your wife, for that which has been begotten in her is of the Holy Spirit.

Luke 3:21-22 And as Jesus was baptized and was praying, heaven was opened, and the Holy Spirit descended in bodily form as a dove upon Him...

WORDS OF MINISTRY: In contrast to Adam, who did not equip himself with God, the Lord Jesus was born a God-man. Because He was conceived of the Holy Spirit, He had the essence of God. In His very being He had the divine essence as His element. He was conceived of this essence, He was born of this essence, and He grew in this essence and lived by it. How marvelous! The Lord was not only full of God—He was God. Because He was God in man, He was the God-man. When the Lord Jesus set Himself aside at the time of His baptism, the economical Spirit descended upon Him to anoint Him. As a result, He was a person both essentially of God and economically for God. Inwardly, He had God as His intrinsic element, and outwardly, He was covered with God as His power. The Man-Savior was full of God inwardly and clothed with God outwardly. As such a person, He was equipped and ready to fight against God's enemy and defeat him. Instead of waiting for the enemy to come to Him, the Lord Jesus, being led of the Spirit, went to the place where the enemy was. The enemy came to the garden to attack Adam, but Jesus went to the wilderness to attack the enemy. When He was led by the Spirit to the wilderness, He was full of God. Thus, He was ready and equipped to deal with the enemy. He went into the wilderness as a warrior and, in the highest standard of morality, He defeated Satan.

Witness Lee, *Life-study of Luke,* pp. 85-86.
(Posted on www.emanna.com on 7/2/2007)

Luke 5:12-13 Behold, there was a man full of leprosy. And when he saw Jesus, he fell on *his* face and begged Him, saying, Lord, if You are willing, You can cleanse me. And stretching out His hand, He touched him, saying, I am willing; be cleansed! And immediately the leprosy left him.

WORDS OF MINISTRY: Here we see that the Man-Savior sympathized with the leper. According to the Old Testament, a leper was not to be touched by anyone. In order to keep others away from him, a leper was required to cry out, "Unclean, unclean!" Hence, a leper was altogether isolated. But the Man-Savior stretched forth His hand to touch this leper. The Lord's touching the leper reveals His human virtue. His divine attributes were expressed in the cleansing of the leper. It is impossible for any human being to cleanse a leper. Therefore, the One who cleansed this leper must be God. In the Lord's sympathy we see His human virtue, and in the cleansing of the leper we see His divine attribute. He was the genuine God-man. As man He was filled with the human virtues, and as God He had the divine attributes that enabled Him to cleanse the man's leprosy. A leper portrays a typical sinner. Leprosy is the most contaminating and damaging disease, isolating its victim both from God and men. To cleanse the leper signifies to recover the sinner to the fellowship with God and with men. It is significant that the leper was not only healed but cleansed. The one with leprosy not only requires healing as those with other diseases; he also needs cleansing, as from sin (1 John 1:7), because of the filthy and contaminating nature of the disease.

Witness Lee, *Life-study of Luke*, pp. 109-110.
(Posted on www.emanna.com on 7/12/2007)

Luke 6:43-44 For there is no good tree that produces corrupt fruit, nor again a corrupt tree that produces good fruit. For each tree is known by its own fruit. For *men* do not collect figs from thorns, nor do they pick grapes from a thornbush.

WORDS OF MINISTRY: In order to practice the principles described in [Luke] 6:17-49, we need the divine life. Life is the basic factor for any kind of being, doing, or working. If we do not have a certain kind of life, we cannot have that kind of being; neither can we have a certain behavior or accomplish a certain work. For example, an apple tree has an apple-tree life. In order for a tree to be an apple tree, it must have the life of an apple tree. Likewise, in order for an animal to be a monkey, it must have the life of a monkey. The crucial point here is that if we would have a certain being and behave in a certain way, we must have a certain kind of life. Life is the basic factor of our being, behavior, and work. The Man-Savior has the kind of life described in chapter 6 of the Gospel of Luke. Before His death and resurrection He Himself lived such a life. But through His resurrection He has become the life-giving Spirit, and now He lives in us. His desire is to live in us the same kind of life He lived on earth. In Philippians 1:21 Paul speaks of living Christ. When Christ, the God-man, was on earth, He lived a life that was according to the highest standard of morality. Now Christ lives in us so that we may live Him. This highest standard of morality is now a person living in us and making it possible for us to live Christ.

Witness Lee, *Life-study of Luke*, pp. 129-130.
(Posted on www.emanna.com on 7/25/2007)

Luke 7:41-42 A certain moneylender had two debtors: one owed five hundred denarii and the other fifty. But since they had nothing *with which* to repay, he graciously forgave them both. Which of them therefore will love him more?

WORDS OF MINISTRY: The Lord's word here indicates that both Simon and the woman were sinners. Simon considered the woman a sinner but did not consider himself a sinner, and he doubted that the Savior knew that she was a sinner. But the Savior's parable indicated that both Simon and the woman were sinners, debtors to Him. According to verse 42, when the two debtors had nothing to repay the moneylender, he graciously forgave them both. This indicates that all sinners have nothing to repay their debt to God their Savior. The Lord's word here also indicates that the Savior had already forgiven them both. The Lord Jesus asked Simon which of the debtors would love the moneylender more as a result of having been forgiven by him. This indicates that love to the Savior is the issue, not the cause, of His forgiveness. In verses 44 through 46 the Lord went on to say to Simon, "Do you see this woman? I entered into your house; you did not give Me water for My feet, but she, with her tears, has wet My feet and with her hair has wiped them. You did not give Me a kiss, but she, from the time I entered, has not stopped kissing My feet affectionately. You did not anoint My head with oil, but she has anointed My feet with ointment." The Savior's word in these verses indicates that Simon should take the woman as an example and learn of her. The great love of the woman was a proof that her many sins had been forgiven. Simon's little love testified that he had experienced forgiveness only a little.

Witness Lee, *Life-study of Luke*, pp. 145-146.
(Posted on www.emanna.com on 8/1/2007)

Luke 7:42-43, 50 But since they had nothing *with which* to repay, he graciously forgave them both. Which of them therefore will love him more? Simon answered and said, I suppose the one whom he graciously forgave the more. And He said to him, You have judged correctly...But He said to the woman, Your faith has saved you. Go in peace.

WORDS OF MINISTRY: When as a young Christian I read this chapter, I thought that the woman's love for the Savior was the cause of the forgiveness of her sins. I thought that He forgave her because she loved Him. This understanding is not correct. In verse 50 the Lord said to the woman that her faith, not her love, had saved her. Furthermore, regarding the two debtors who were forgiven by the moneylender, the Lord asked, "Which of them therefore will love him more?" (v. 42). This indicates clearly that love is the issue of forgiveness. Concerning this, we need to pay attention to the word *therefore* in verse 42. This word proves that love comes after forgiveness instead of preceding it. What, then, is the cause of the forgiveness of sins? From verse 50 we see that the cause is faith. It was the woman's faith that saved her. Her sins were forgiven not because of her love but because of her faith. Therefore, faith comes before forgiveness, and love follows faith. It is very important for us to see that forgiveness comes before love. We should not think that our love is the cause of the forgiveness of our sins. On the contrary, love is the issue, the outcome, of our faith. When we believe in the Lord, our faith becomes the cause of the Lord's forgiveness of our sins. Then as a result of having our sins forgiven, we begin to love the Lord. Hence, love comes out of faith.

Witness Lee, *Life-study of Luke*, pp. 147-148.
(Posted on www.emanna.com on 8/2/2007)

Faith, Love, and Peace (3)

Luke 7:47-50 For this reason I say to you, Her sins which are many are forgiven, because she loved much; but to whom little is forgiven, he loves little. And He said to her, Your sins are forgiven. And those who were reclining *at table* with *Him* began to say within themselves, Who is this who even forgives sins? But He said to the woman, Your faith has saved you. Go in peace.

WORDS OF MINISTRY: Love issues in peace. First we believe in the Lord Jesus, having faith in Him. Then we are forgiven of all our sins, and this brings in love for the Lord. As we love Him, this love issues in peace. We, then, may walk in peace. To walk in peace means to live in peace, to have a life of peace. When we walk in peace, we have our being in peace and live a peaceful life. This means that when we believe in the Lord, we love Him and live a life in peace. This is the Christian life. As those who love the Lord, we live, walk, and have our being in peace. The atmosphere in 7:36-50 is an atmosphere of affection. There is affection both on the side of the Man-Savior and on the side of the sinful woman. The Lord's affection is an aspect of His human virtues. Once again in His human virtues we can see His divine attributes. In particular, we see the attribute of divine authority to forgive a person's sins. This One is the very God, for He alone has the authority to forgive sins. The Man-Savior's divine attributes are also shown in His giving peace to the forgiven sinner. Only God can give peace to a forgiven sinner. Are you able to give peace to others? It is not in our hand to give others peace. Peace is in the almighty hand of God. Only He can forgive sins and give peace. Therefore, the forgiving of sins and the giving of peace are two attributes of God. Here these attributes are expressed in the Savior's human virtues.

Witness Lee, *Life-study of Luke*, pp. 148-149.
(Posted on www.emanna.com on 8/3/2007)